Review of a Model to Assess Stranding of Juvenile Salmon by Ship Wakes along the Lower Columbia River, Oregon and Washington

By Tobias J. Kock, John M. Plumb, and Noah S. Adams

Prepared in cooperation with the U.S. Army Corps of Engineers

Open-File Report 2013–1229

U.S. Department of the Interior
U.S. Geological Survey

U.S. Department of the Interior
SALLY JEWELL, Secretary

U.S. Geological Survey
Suzette M. Kimball, Acting Director

U.S. Geological Survey, Reston, Virginia: 2013

For more information on the USGS—the Federal source for science about the Earth,
its natural and living resources, natural hazards, and the environment—visit
http://www.usgs.gov or call 1–888–ASK–USGS

For an overview of USGS information products, including maps, imagery, and publications,
visit http://www.usgs.gov/pubprod

To order this and other USGS information products, visit http://store.usgs.gov

Suggested citation:
Kock, T.J., Plumb, J.M., and Adams, N.S., 2013, Review of a model to assess stranding of juvenile salmon by ship
wakes along the Lower Columbia River, Oregon and Washington: U.S. Geological Survey Open-File Report 2013-
1129, 20 p., http://pubs.usgs.gov/of/2013/1229.

Contents

Figure

Tables

iii

Conversion Factors

Inch/Pound to SI

Multiply	By	To obtain
	Length	
foot (ft)	0.3048	meter (m)
cubic foot per second (ft^3/s)	0.02832	cubic meter per second (m^3/s)

Review of a Model to Assess Stranding of Juvenile Salmon by Ship Wakes along the Lower Columbia River, Oregon and Washington

By Tobias J. Kock, John M. Plumb, and Noah S. Adams

Executive Summary

Long period wake waves from deep draft vessels have been shown to strand small fish, particularly juvenile Chinook salmon *Oncorhynchus tschawytcha*, in the lower Columbia River (LCR). The U.S. Army Corps of Engineers is responsible for maintaining the shipping channel in the LCR and recently conducted dredging operations to deepen the shipping channel from an authorized depth of 40 feet (ft) to an authorized depth of 43 ft (in areas where rapid shoaling was expected, dredging operations were used to increase the channel depth to 48 ft). A model was developed to estimate stranding probabilities for juvenile salmon under the 40- and 43-ft channel scenarios, to determine if channel deepening was going to affect wake stranding (Assessment of potential stranding of juvenile salmon by ship wakes along the Lower Columbia River under scenarios of ship traffic and channel depth: Report prepared for the Portland District U.S. Army Corps of Engineers, Portland, Oregon). The U.S. Army Corps of Engineers funded the U.S. Geological Survey to review this model. A total of 30 review questions were provided to guide the review process, and these questions are addressed in this report. In general, we determined that the analyses by Pearson (2011) were appropriate given the data available. We did identify two areas where additional information could have been provided: (1) a more thorough description of model diagnostics and model selection would have been useful for the reader to better understand the model framework; and (2) model uncertainty should have been explicitly described and reported in the document. Stranding probability estimates between the 40- and 43-ft channel depths were minimally different under most of the scenarios that were examined by Pearson (2011), and a discussion of the effects of uncertainty given these minimal differences would have been useful. Ultimately, however, a stochastic (or simulation) model would provide the best opportunity to illustrate uncertainty within a given set of model predictions, but such an approach would require a substantial amount of additional data collection. Several review questions focused on the accuracy and precision of the model estimates, but we were unable to address these questions because of the limited data that currently exists regarding wake stranding in the LCR. Additional field studies will be required to validate findings from Pearson (2011), if concerns regarding accuracy and precision remain a priority. Although the Pearson (2011) model provided a useful examination of stranding under pre-construction and post-construction conditions, future research will be required to better understand the effects of wake stranding on juvenile salmonids throughout the entire LCR. If additional information on wake stranding is desired in the future, the following topics may be of interest: (1) spatial examination of wake stranding throughout the entire LCR; (2) additional evaluation of juvenile salmonid behavior and population dynamics; (3) assessing and integrating predicted changes in ship development; and (4) assessing and integrating predicted changes in climate on environmental factors known to cause stranding.

Section 1: Background

The U.S. Army Corps of Engineers (USACE) is responsible for maintaining the shipping channel in the lower Columbia River (LCR). The LCR shipping channel has historically been maintained (through dredging) at an authorized depth of 40 ft, but a channel deepening project was proposed in the mid-2000s to increase the authorized depth to 43 ft, thereby allowing ships to load to a deeper draft for transit in the LCR. The intent was to provide an economic benefit by increasing shipping efficiency in the LCR. However, increased vessel size and draft have the potential to negatively affect juvenile salmon *Oncorhynchus* spp. populations in the LCR.

Research has shown that ship wakes can wash juvenile salmon onto beaches where they can be stranded and die. Bauersfeld (1977) monitored LCR beaches between Vancouver, Washington, and the Cowlitz River (53 river kilometers [rkm]) and estimated that nearly 152,000 juvenile salmon were killed by wake stranding during February–July 1975. However, Hinton and Emmett (1994) studied wake stranding of juvenile salmon in the LCR during 1992–1993 and found only 11 stranded fish during their study. The authors concluded that "stranding of juvenile salmonids is not presently a significant cause of juvenile salmonid mortality in the lower Columbia River (Hinton and Emmett, 1994, p. iii)." In a more recent study, Ackerman (2002) observed high variation in the number of fish stranded by wakes, and concluded that the discrepancy between his study and those that were previously conducted (Bauersfeld, 1977; Hinton and Emmett, 1994) would require further studies with a carefully constructed sample design to accurately assess the causes of vessel wake-induced stranding of juvenile salmonids.

Based on the available information at the time, the National Marine Fisheries Service (NMFS) concluded in their Biological Opinion on the USACE's Columbia River Channel Improvements Project (hereafter referred to as the BIOP; National Marine Fisheries Service, 2002) that "the proposed action (channel deepening) is not likely to jeopardize the continued existence of the 13 ESA-listed species potentially affected by the Project, or result in the destruction or adverse modification of designated critical habitat (p. 43)." However, the BIOP did call for a study to be conducted before and after channel deepening to determine if the deepening of the channel resulted in increased stranding of juvenile salmon in the LCR. To meet the BIOP requirement, the USACE contracted with the Pacific Northwest National Laboratory (PNNL) during 2004 and 2005 to conduct research on pre-channel-deepening stranding rates (Pearson and others, 2006). Construction to deepen the channel took place in stages from 2005 to 2010. Post-construction monitoring actions are scheduled to be completed in 2013.

The USACE convened an Adaptive Management Team (AMT) that was tasked with the planning and decision-making associated with preventing, reducing, or mitigating environmental impacts from the channel deepening project. Recently, the AMT has questioned whether results from a post-deepening study would be able to determine if the deepening of the channel resulted in increased stranding of juvenile salmon in the LCR, or if resources might be better used if applied to other activities such as additional research and/or pilot projects to reduce stranding. The USACE funded Peapod Research, a consulting firm, to develop a report and model for the AMT. The goal of the report was to summarize the current state of knowledge regarding stranding, and the model was designed to estimate stranding probabilities under several different ship-traffic scenarios in pre-deepening and post-deepening channels of the LCR. This report and model were developed and presented to the AMT in

2011 (Pearson, 2011). Results from this effort are important components in the decision-making process for the AMT regarding whether or not a post-deepening study should be conducted. Given the importance of this information, the AMT requested a third-party review of the Pearson (2011) model and report. The U.S. Geological Survey was funded to complete the review, and this report summarizes findings from that review process. The AMT developed a list of 30 questions they wanted addressed during the review of the Pearson (2011) report and model. Each of the questions is addressed in the following sections of this report.

Section 2: Model Description

Section 2.1: Is the Pearson (2011) model, including the approach, methods, and data, described and summarized in a readily understood and transparent manner?

The Pearson (2011) report is concise, well-written, and provided good information regarding wake stranding of juvenile salmon in the LCR. The report summarized previous findings from other studies and provided background information that informed the reader on what was currently known about wake stranding in the LCR. The author described how the 2011 model was developed as an adaptation of a model that was previously used for determining which factors were important in wake stranding of juvenile salmon (Pearson and others, 2006; Pearson and Skalski, 2011). Pearson (2011) succinctly described and summarized the approach used to estimate stranding probabilities under two channel-depth conditions (pre-construction depth of 40 ft; post-construction depth of 43 ft). The model description explained that the model included nine parameters (table 1). Although much of the report contained sufficient information for assessing the model and the model results, we did identify areas where additional information may have been useful.

Table 1. Parameters and parameter estimates from Pearson (2011), and analyses conducted by the U.S. Geological Survey (USGS) to complete the model review that is described in this report.

[Parameters include sampling locations at Barlow Point (BP), County Line Park (CL), and Sauvie Island (SI), ship length (L), cross-section ratio of the river channel (XS), ship speed ($speed^2$), juvenile salmon density, river flow, and tide height). Numbers in parentheses are standard error estimates. Parameters that were transformed using the natural log are identified by ln]

Variable	Pearson estimates	USGS estimates
Intercept (BP)	-32.599	-32.430 (16.832)
Location 2 (CL)	-2.720	-2.688 (0.914)
Location 3 (SI)	-1.190	-1.187 (0.656)
ln (L)	3.901	3.879 (2.260)
ln (XS)	1.125	1.117 (1.294)
ln ($speed^2$)	2.209	2.200 (0.882)
Juvenile salmon density	0.111	0.110 (0.004)
River flow	-0.0000035	-0.0000035 (0.0000025)
Tide height	-0.564	-0.562 (0.029)

The dataset that was used to estimate parameter values for the model was not clearly described in the report, which limited the reader's ability to understand the limitations that might exist when interpreting findings from the study. Pearson (2011) referenced a previous report (Pearson and others, 2006) that contained information about the dataset that was collected at the following LCR locations:

1. Barlow Point (river mile [RM] 62);
2. County Line Park (RM 51); and
3. Sauvie Island (RM 97).

Data collection occurred during summer 2004, winter 2005, and spring 2005, and a total of 126 vessel-passage events were observed. During each vessel-passage event, data were recorded for 19 different variables. The appendixes summarized the data collected during this period, but it was not clear to the reader if all or only some of the data were used to determine parameter estimates in the model. Although the master dataset included information from all 126 vessel-passage events, there were missing data records for some of the variables. In several cases, information for individual vessels was not available, which precluded calculations required for some of the parameters in the model. For instance, when ship dimensions were not available, it was not possible to determine ship length, or to calculate the cross-section ratio that requires information about ship draft and ship beam dimensions. There also were missing records for salmon density and ship speed, which are parameters in the model. Ultimately, the missing data resulted in 77 percent (97 of 126 data records; hereafter referred to as the "reduced dataset") of the original dataset being useful for estimating model parameters. Although it was possible for the reader to review various components of the dataset in the appendixes, it would have been useful to clearly summarize which data were used when obtaining parameter estimates for the model.

We examined the reduced dataset and observed that, in some cases, the sampling strategy used for collecting data may have resulted in a dataset that was lacking a representative sample at the study sites. For example, 15 ship-passage events were present in the reduced dataset from the summer sampling period at Barlow Point (table 2). More than one-half (53 percent; 8 of 15 daily records) of the river-flow data from the summer sampling period at Barlow Point occurred during a single day, which means that river flows on that day (163,000 ft^3/s) made a substantial contribution to the flow dataset. Similarly, 64 percent (7 of 11 records) of the ship passage events observed during the winter at Sauvie Island occurred during periods when the tide was incoming, so negative river flow values comprised a larger percentage of the data records compared to the other sampling sites (table 2). These examples are provided because this information is often insightful for readers when interpreting model results. They provide information about potential shortcomings of the dataset and suggest that the scope of inference for the findings may be limited, but do not suggest that any of the findings from Pearson (2011) were biased or invalid.

Table 2. Daily river flow data from Pearson (2011) that is grouped by season and sampling location.

[Negative river flows in the lower Columbia River can occur during incoming tidal periods. Units of measure for river flows are cubic feet per second]

Summer			Winter			Spring		
Sauvie Island	Barlow Point	County Line Park	Sauvie Island	Barlow Point	County Line Park	Sauvie Island	Barlow Point	County Line Park
147,000	204,000	205,000	98,600	255,000	70,400	330,000	335,000	362,000
154,000	125,000	205,000	-116,000	-93,500	-46,000	302,000	321,000	357,000
145,000	147,000	205,000	-94,400	12,200	-55,000	300,000	191,000	324,000
145,000	147,000	137,000	-51,900	303,000	11,800	374,000	116,000	236,000
122,000	153,000	137,000	-51,900	340,000	105,000	373,000	314,000	447,000
122,000	174,000	107,000	-20,100	267,000	3,920	377,000	451,000	358,000
122,000	174,000	107,000	-101,000	234,000	25,400	359,000	450,000	427,000
122,000	163,000	129,000	-119,000	75,000	179,000	356,000	363,000	
121,000	163,000	129,000	261,000	273,000	271,000	410,000	345,000	
121,000	163,000	153,000	231,000	75,100	297,000	414,000		
	163,000		265,000	289,000	-79,300	300,000		
	163,000					414,000		
	163,000							
	163,000							
	163,000							

Section 2.2: Was the model designed and executed with sufficient detail to permit evaluation of its technical quality?

Pearson (2011) did not provide a detailed description of diagnostic tests that were performed on the model, or detailed accounts of the model selection process. Model development generally involves a series of steps to determine which parameters should be included in the model, and which models provide the best fit to the data. This process is important because it provides insights regarding potential sources of uncertainty and bias, and allows the reader to assess the quality of the model that is ultimately used. Pearson (2011) provided information about the predictive capability of the model by reporting the Goodman-Kruskal Gamma statistic, however, he did not provide additional information about model diagnostics or model selection, and these descriptions would have been very useful for assessing the model. For example, parameters such as ship length, ship speed, and river cross-section ratio could contain similar information and create collinearity issues for the model. When collinearity is a problem, parameter estimates can be unstable, and standard error values are often inflated (Quinn and Keogh, 2002). We examined a correlation matrix and variance inflation factors to determine if collinearity was an issue for the Pearson (2011) model. In some cases, these tests can yield conflicting results. For example, correlation values ranged from 0.031 to 0.601 (table 3), which indicated that collinearity was not problematic. However, variance inflation factor values were all greater than 10.0, which could indicate a problem with collinearity (table 4). These results suggested that collinearity could potentially affect results from the model, so we conducted additional diagnostic tests to examine this factor. These diagnostic tests did not identify issues with the results that were caused by collinearity. The lack of documentation on the assessment of model fit also excluded descriptions of how, or if, overdispersion and binomial error were assessed, and these are common problems with models (Burnham and Anderson, 2002). Descriptions regarding model selection would also have provided additional information about how the final model for fish stranding was selected. For example, model selection using Akaike's information criterion (AIC) is a commonly used technique (Burnham and Anderson, 2002) for comparing how various models fit a particular dataset.

Contemporary statistical packages produce a single AIC value for each model, and this value can be compared to AIC values of other models to determine which model best fits the data. The model with the lowest AIC value provides the best fit to the data and the difference in AIC values (that is, ΔAIC) between the best-fitting model and other models provides a relative measure of model plausibility. Burnham and Anderson (2002) suggest that when ΔAIC values range from 0 to 2, there is equivocal support for either model. Conversely, when ΔAIC values range from 4 to 7, there is considerably less support for the model with the higher AIC value. If ΔAIC values are greater than 10, there is essentially no support for the model with the higher AIC value. We created some example results of different models to demonstrate how the AIC model selection process can be used to provide insight into the way the final and "best" model is chosen. For this analysis we used AIC_c, which is an adaptation of AIC that accounts for small sample sizes (Burnham and Anderson, 2002). Table 5 shows AIC_c model selection results for five models. Models 1, 4, and 5 are adaptations of the Pearson (2011) model that we created.

Table 3. Correlation matrix for parameters from Pearson (2011).

[Parameters that were transformed using the natural log are identified by ln]

Parameter	ln(Ship length)	ln(Cross-section ratio)	ln(Ship speed)	Salmon density	River flow	Tide height
ln(Ship length)	1.000	0.601	0.138	-0.139	-0.031	-0.083
ln(Cross-section ratio)	0.601	1.000	0.204	-0.019	0.068	-0.127
ln(Ship speed)	0.138	0.204	1.000	0.139	0.272	0.120
Salmon density	-0.139	-0.019	0.139	1.000	0.426	-0.120
River flow	-0.031	0.068	0.272	0.426	1.000	-0.489
Tide height	-0.083	-0.127	0.120	-0.120	-0.489	1.000

Table 4. Variance inflation factors for parameters from Pearson (2011).

[Parameters that were transformed using the natural log are identified by ln]

Variable	Variance inflation factor value
ln(Ship length)	12.97
ln(Cross-section ratio)	14.82
ln(Ship speed)	11.66
Salmon density	10.94
River flow	12.56
Tide height	16.46

Table 5. Model selection table comparing five models.

[Models 1, 4, and 5 are adaptations of the Pearson (2011) model. Model 2 is the Pearson (2011) model. Model 3 is the Pearson (2006) model. K-1 refers to the number of parameters in each model. AIC$_c$ refers to Akaikes's information criterion with a correction for small sample sizes. Parameters that were transformed using the natural log are identified by ln]

Model No.	Parameters	K-1	AIC$_c$ value	ΔAIC$_c$
1	Intercept (BP), Location 2 (CL), Location 3 (SI), ln(Ship Length), ln(Ship Speed^2),Salmon Density, River Flow, Tide Height	8	100.18	0.00
2	Intercept (BP), Location 2 (CL), Location 3 (SI), ln(Ship Length), ln(Cross-Section Ratio), ln(Ship Speed^2), Salmon Density, River Flow, Tide Height	9	101.40	1.22
3	Intercept (BP), Location 2 (CL), Location 3 (SI), Kinetic Energy Proxy (KEP), Tide Height, Salmon Density, KEP X Tide Height, Salmon Density X Tide Height	8	101.79	1.61
4	Intercept (BP), Location 2 (CL), Location 3 (SI), Salmon Density, River Flow	5	104.22	4.04
5	Intercept (BP), Location 2 (CL), Location 3 (SI), ln(Cross-Section Ratio), Salmon Density, River Flow, Tide Height	7	107.22	7.04

Model 2 is the model Pearson presented in his 2011 report, and model 3 is a different model that Pearson presented in 2006. To create model 1, we removed the cross-section ratio parameter from the model Pearson reported in 2011. By removing this parameter, the model we created appears to fit the data slightly better (ΔAIC$_c$ = 1.22) than the Pearson (2011) model. This does not suggest that model 1 should have been used instead of the Pearson (2011) model. Rather, it indicates that cross-section ratio was not an important predictor of stranding probability. However, this parameter was necessary to meet the modeling objectives of comparing pre- and post-deepening effects on fish stranding. To create models 4 and 5 for this example, we removed several additional parameters from the model that Pearson presented in 2011. In both cases, the AIC$_c$ valued showed that the Pearson (2011) model fit the data better than model 4 and 5 (that is, ΔAIC$_c$ values are greater than 4.0). We provided these examples to illustrate how inclusion of the model selection results could have helped the reader better understand how the best model was selected and the relative importance each parameter had to the best fitting model.

A description of how the model was used to evaluate various scenarios requested by the AMT was provided in the section, "Appendixes" of the Pearson (2011) report. This information was thorough. The author provided great detail and supporting data for the various scenarios provided clear information regarding how the parameters were estimated, and provided the data that were input into the model. This aspect of the report was very explicit and useful for the reader.

Section 2.3: Are any additional descriptions or details needed for a potential user to understand and/or apply the model? If so, what additional information might be needed?

We attempted to apply the Pearson (2011) model to the reduced dataset in order to validate findings from the report and were initially able to reproduce parameter estimates for all variables except salmon density. Although there was a substantial amount of salmon density data in appendix A of the report, it was not clear from the description in the report which data were used to obtain parameter estimates. For example, we could not determine if the salmon density parameter was estimated using data from subyearling Chinook salmon *O. tshawytscha* (0+ Chinook in appendix A), total salmonid density, daily average density, seasonal average density, or other data. We contacted the author and learned that total salmonid density was used to estimate the salmon density parameter. Once this information was obtained, we were able to replicate all parameter estimates from the Pearson (2011) model. Based on this observation, we suggest that the report could have included explicit descriptions of the data that were included in the logistic regression model. This information would expedite the process of applying the model for a potential user who was previously unfamiliar with the model and dataset. We also observed that the author did not provide information about the uncertainty associated with estimating the parameters, or the uncertainty associated with the estimates of stranding probabilities. This information was critical for interpreting the findings from the study. We have included standard errors for parameter estimates in table 1, and address issues associated with uncertainty in greater detail in Section 4 of this report.

Section 3: Model Credibility and Suitability for Analysis

Section 3.1: Is the resulting mathematical and statistical structure of the fish stranding model (that is, Pearson, 2011) scientifically credible and technically defensible?

We examined the wake stranding model by: (1) conducting a series of model diagnostic tests, (2) evaluating a set of candidate models that could also be used to describe the data, and (3) attempting to replicate the findings in the report using a different statistical software package. We did not identify any issues that would suggest that the model was not scientifically credible or technically defensible. Furthermore, we were able to replicate parameter estimates and model outputs using the same dataset, but a different statistical software package. Pearson (2011) used software called Minitab, and we used software called R. Based on this review process, we conclude that the author's application of a logistic regression model was appropriate for the analyses.

Section 3.2: Does the model formulation logically derive from the design and results of the pre-project stranding studies on which the model is based?

The model presented in the 2011 report was developed as an adaptation of a previously reported model (Pearson and others, 2006; Pearson and Skalski, 2007) used to identify factors that affected the wake stranding of juvenile salmon in the LCR. Both models shared five common parameters: (1) the intercept, which refers to the Barlow Point sampling location; (2) location 2, which refers to the County Line Park sampling location; (3) location 3, which refers to the Sauvie Island sampling location; (4) tidal height; and (5) salmon density. The 2006 model also included a kinetic energy proxy (KEP) parameter, and two interaction parameters (KEP × tidal height; salmon density × tidal height). The formula used to calculate KEP is:

$$KEP = (\text{vessel length} \times \text{vessel beam} \times \text{vessel draft}) \times \text{vessel speed}^2 \times 10^{-8} \qquad (1)$$

Although the 2006 and 2011 models used slightly different parameters, both models incorporated the same type of data. The calculation of KEP for the 2006 model incorporates vessel length and vessel speed, which are individual parameters in the 2011 model. Similarly, vessel beam and vessel draft data are incorporated into the cross-section ratio parameter for the 2011 model and in the KEP parameter in the 2006 model. The ship length, cross-section ratio, and ship speed parameters included a natural log transformation. This is a common statistical procedure but the reasons for doing so are not clearly described in Pearson (2011). River flow is the only parameter that is included in the 2011 model but is not included in the 2006 model. Our model selection analysis found that both the 2006 and 2011 models fit the data equally well because the ΔAIC_c between the two models (table 5; models 2 and 3) is 0.39. Given that both models used similar data and provided similar fit to the data, we conclude that the 2011 model was appropriate in design, given what is known from previous studies of wake stranding in the LCR, but more description would have been useful in Pearson (2011).

Section 3.3: Have the previously developed supporting data concerning stranding in the LCR been properly used in developing the Pearson (2011) statistical stranding model?

The supporting data were used appropriately to develop the model describing stranding at three sites in the LCR, not the LCR as a whole. See Section 3.1 and 3.2 in this report for additional observations that support this finding.

Section 3.4: Are the stated assumptions underlying the Pearson (2011) model development and application reasonable and defensible?

The analysis of the model was based on three general assumptions. The first assumption was that the dataset, which was collected during 2004–2005, adequately represented the range of conditions that occur at Barlow Point, County Line Park, and Sauvie Island. The second assumption was that the scenarios developed for analysis are realistic comparisons between pre-construction and post-construction conditions in the LCR. The third assumption was that results from the analysis were only applicable to Barlow Point, County Line Park, and Sauvie Island. The primary goal of the Pearson (2011) analysis was to use a logistic regression model to predict how stranding probabilities would change between the pre-construction and post-construction LCR, given the assumptions stated above.

We previously discussed several aspects of the dataset with regards to sample size and variability. Pearson (2011) addresses similar concerns in the section, "Discussion" of his report, but this does not suggest that the findings from the study are biased or inaccurate. We observed that the reduced dataset included less than 100 vessel passage events. We identified areas where the variability in this dataset may be somewhat limited with regards to natural conditions (Section 2.1 in this report). Pearson (2011) explained that river flow data less than 450,000 ft^3/s were not present in the dataset used for analysis, and cautioned that findings from the study should not be extrapolated beyond the range of the data. Additionally, data used in this analysis were all collected prior to channel deepening, therefore data that are relevant to post-deepening conditions were not collected or analyzed. This is an important observation because the post-deepening results are essential for predicting how channel deepening might affect wake stranding. These findings do not suggest that the assumptions of Pearson (2011) are unreasonable or indefensible, but rather are a reminder that the analysis was constrained by the data. Given this observation, the Pearson (2011) analysis was valid and provided a useful examination of the effect that altered channel depth had on stranding probabilities at three locations.

The second assumption was reasonable and defensible given that the scenarios were based on expected changes in shipping trends once channel deepening was complete. Pearson (2011) provided thorough descriptions of these scenarios. For example, scenario 2 used published predictions for future ship traffic forecasts (U.S. Army Corps of Engineers, 2003) and also considered advanced dredging requirements in which the shipping channel was dredged to a depth of 48 ft where rapid shoaling was anticipated (Pearson, 2011).

Pearson (2011) suggested that findings from his study could be applicable to areas of the LCR other than Barlow Point, County Line Park, and Sauvie Island. However, the author also clearly stated that these areas represent only a small portion of the LCR where fish stranding may occur. Pearson (2011) used information from a previous study (Pearson and others, 2008) to determine that about 11 percent of the beaches in the LCR may exhibit fish stranding levels similar to those observed during the

9

Pearson (2011) study. The author stated that "model outcomes cannot be extrapolated to the whole of the LCR" (Pearson, 2011). Given these observations, the reader clearly understands that the model outcomes are based on data collected from just three sampling locations, and thus should not be considered representative of the entire LCR. Each of the three basic assumptions of the Pearson (2011) model has been discussed. These assumptions appear reasonable and defensible given the dataset used for the analysis and the goals of the study.

Section 3.5: Are the model assumptions justified in relation to the design and results of the pre-project stranding studies and the general understanding of conditions and processes important in fish stranding in the Lower Columbia River and estuary?

This question is nearly identical to the question addressed in Section 3.4 of this report, thus we refer the reader to that section for responses relevant to this question.

Section 3.6: Are the selected commercial navigation scenarios analyzed using the model representative of current post-project and projected future navigation, as described in the National Marine Fisheries Service's Columbia River Channel Improvements Project Biological Opinion, on the Lower Columbia River and estuary?

The scenarios that were analyzed by Pearson (2011) included a range of characteristics that are consistent with future navigation projections. Projecting future navigation trends is difficult because these trends are affected by factors such as commerce-related needs, technological development, and other factors that are difficult to anticipate and account for. Two documents, U.S. Army Corps of Engineers (2003) and National Marine Fisheries Service (2002), provide general forecasts that were apparently used in scenario development by Pearson (2011). The assessed scenarios are consistent with forecasts from these documents. More importantly, Pearson (2011) has developed a system that can be efficiently used to assess additional scenarios if future navigation trends are altered or of interest.

Section 3.7: Are the methods of data analysis suitable for estimating stranding probability?

We conducted a thorough review of Pearson (2011) and found that his application of a logistic regression model for estimating several stranding probability scenarios was suitable and appropriate. During our review process, we conducted a thorough assessment of the literature and reviewed the Pearson (2011) report regarding wake stranding in the LCR. We obtained data directly from the author, and replicated his findings. Throughout this document, we provide commentary on additional information that could have been incorporated in Pearson (2011). These comments are intended to be constructive and provide additional information for the reader interested in the details of the analysis. In general, we determined that the analyses by Pearson (2011) to be appropriate and valid.

Section 3.8: Was the model used correctly in the analysis of stranding?

This question is nearly identical to the question posed in Section 3.7 of this report, thus we refer the reader to that section for responses relevant to this question.

Section 3.9: Have the resulting model parameters been accurately and reliably estimated?

It is not clear if this question refers to the correct calculation of the model parameters given the model structure and dataset, or if this refers to the accuracy and reliability of the parameter estimates with respect to actual (true) wake stranding trends in the LCR. We conducted a parallel analysis using the Pearson (2011) model and dataset, and were able to obtain parameter estimates that were nearly identical (table 1) to those reported. This suggests that the Pearson (2011) calculated parameter estimates were correct given the structure of the model and the data that were used. However, the term "accuracy" is often used in science and statistics to describe how close a parameter estimate is to the actual (true) measurement of that variable in the system being studied. Similarly, the term "reliable" is used to describe how precise the estimates are with respect to truth. With respect to these definitions, we cannot provide an assessment of the accuracy and reliability of the Pearson (2011) parameter estimates because wake stranding is still not completely understood in the LCR, and the available data were too sparse to allow this type of assessment. A validation study could be conducted to collect additional field data at Barlow Point, County Line Park, and Sauvie Island, and these data could be compared to model predictions to assess the accuracy and reliability of the Pearson (2011) estimates if this type of assessment is truly desired.

Section 4: Model Results and Conclusions

Section 4.1: Are the inferences and conclusions drawn from the model results concerning stranding probability reasonable, particularly in relation to estimated percentage changes in stranding potential?

Pearson (2011) used a credible model and data to predict how stranding probabilities at Barlow Point, County Line Park, and Sauvie Island might change as a result of the LCR's channel deepening from 40- to 43-ft deep, and the results from these efforts are reasonable and well supported. Previous sections in this report have addressed the credibility of the model and the approach used by Pearson (2011). We confirmed various calculations made during his analyses to verify that the reported findings were correct. Given these considerations, the results appear to be reasonable and appropriate for the objectives of the study. Pearson (2011) determined that increases in channel depth would primarily result in slight decreases in stranding probabilities at the study sites. The exceptions to these findings were scenarios that included large container ships. When these vessels were examined in the analysis, the model results suggested that stranding probabilities would increase slightly. Finally, we observed that Pearson (2011) provided clear support for inferences and conclusions that were made in the document, and the limitations of these conclusions were clearly stated, in most cases.

One aspect of the study that was not addressed by Pearson (2011) was the effect of uncertainty on stranding probability estimates obtained during the analysis. This issue is very important with regards to inferences and conclusions that were made in the document. Uncertainty is thoroughly addressed in Section 4.4 of this report and we refer the reader to that section for more information on the topic.

Section 4.2: Given the structure of the stranding model, its underlying assumptions, and supporting data, how accurate are the projected changes in the probabilities of fish stranding?

Existing data for wake stranding in the LCR are relatively sparse, and studies that have been conducted on the topic have frequently yielded conflicting conclusions, so it is not currently possible to assess the accuracy of Pearson's (2011) probability estimates. Studies focusing on wake stranding in the LCR have been conducted by Bauersfeld (1977), Emmett and others (1993), Hinton and Emmett (1994), Ackermann (2002), Pearson and others (2006), Pearson and Skalski (2007), Pearson (2011), and Pearson and Skalksi (2011). This list seems to suggest that a substantial amount of work has been conducted on wake stranding in the LCR, but most of the listed research has been focused on select

11

locations in the LCR, and several of the studies have used existing data rather than collecting new data. For example, Pearson and others (2006), Pearson and Skalski (2007), Pearson (2011), and Pearson and Skalksi (2011) have all used a single dataset, which has previously been described in this report. Additionally, none of the studies collected substantial amounts of data throughout the LCR, which has likely resulted in conflicting conclusions in several cases. For example, Hinton and Emmett (1994) concluded that "stranding of juvenile salmonids is not presently a significant source of juvenile salmonid mortality in the LCR (p. iii)." Conversely, Pearson and Skalski (2007) estimated that as many as 42,605 juvenile salmonids could be stranded at Barlow Point, County Line Park, and Sauvie Island in a single year. Additionally, most studies of wake stranding in the LCR have focused on Barlow Point, County Line Park, and Sauvie Island, so little information currently exists for other locations throughout the LCR. Given these observations, we conclude that wake stranding in the LCR is not thoroughly understood, which precludes our ability to assess whether or not findings from Pearson (2011) are accurate. To better assess the findings of Pearson (2011), additional field work would be required to collect data that would be used for validating findings from the study.

Section 4.3: Does the Pearson (2011) model and its application appear biased towards overestimating or underestimating probabilities of fish stranding?

Pearson (2011) provided some information regarding overestimating and underestimating the probabilities of fish stranding in table 15 of his report. This was based on comparisons between output from the 2011 model and observed data from the 2004–2005 dataset. This information was insightful and useful for the reader. However, these results were constrained by the available data, and should not be interpreted to represent a comparison between model results and truth. To evaluate this more effectively, Pearson (2011) could have withheld a portion of the data when fitting the model and then compared the output to this data. However, this was not done, and the dataset was small to begin with, as previously discussed. Therefore, we cannot determine if the Pearson (2011) model was biased and overestimated or underestimated wake stranding in the LCR. Readers are referred to Section 3.9 and Section 4.2 for additional discussion on this topic.

Section 4.4: What are the implications of parameter uncertainty on the accuracy and precision of the model results given the structure of the empirical model?

Pearson (2011) did not provide a detailed discussion of parameter uncertainty in his report, but this factor is important when interpreting his findings. For most scenarios, Pearson (2011) reported relatively small (< 5 percent) changes in stranding probabilities between pre-dredged and post-dredged scenarios. These probability estimates did not include standard errors or confidence intervals so the reader could not gauge how much uncertainty was associated with each estimate. We provided standard errors for parameter estimates in table 1 of this report, and included an illustration of stranding probability estimates with 95-percent confidence intervals for a subset of the data (fig. 1). We plotted stranding probability estimates from Scenario 1 for bulk carriers that were departing (moving downstream) and included estimates for all three beaches during spring, summer, and winter (fig. 1). Figure 1 supports observations made by Pearson (2011) in regards to the slight differences in stranding probability estimates between the two channel depths. However, the slight differences between stranding probability estimates are overshadowed by large confidence intervals for each estimate (fig. 1). Confidence intervals overlap almost completely for each pair of estimates, suggesting no difference between the estimates. The goal of the Pearson (2011) research was to describe how wake stranding would be affected by the channel deepening. Our illustration represents the worst case scenario for this analysis because data are presented by sampling location and season (fig. 1). Although pooling data across seasons to report differences in stranding probabilities at each site between pre-construction and post-construction conditions would reduce the uncertainty because of the larger sample size, it is important to understand that uncertainty must be considered when examining findings from Pearson (2011) because the predicted differences in stranding probabilities are consistently small, and the shortcomings of the dataset (which were previously described) result in rather large confidence intervals for each estimate. The use of a simulation model (discussed in Section 5.1 of this report) would provide the best approach for evaluating uncertainty in this case.

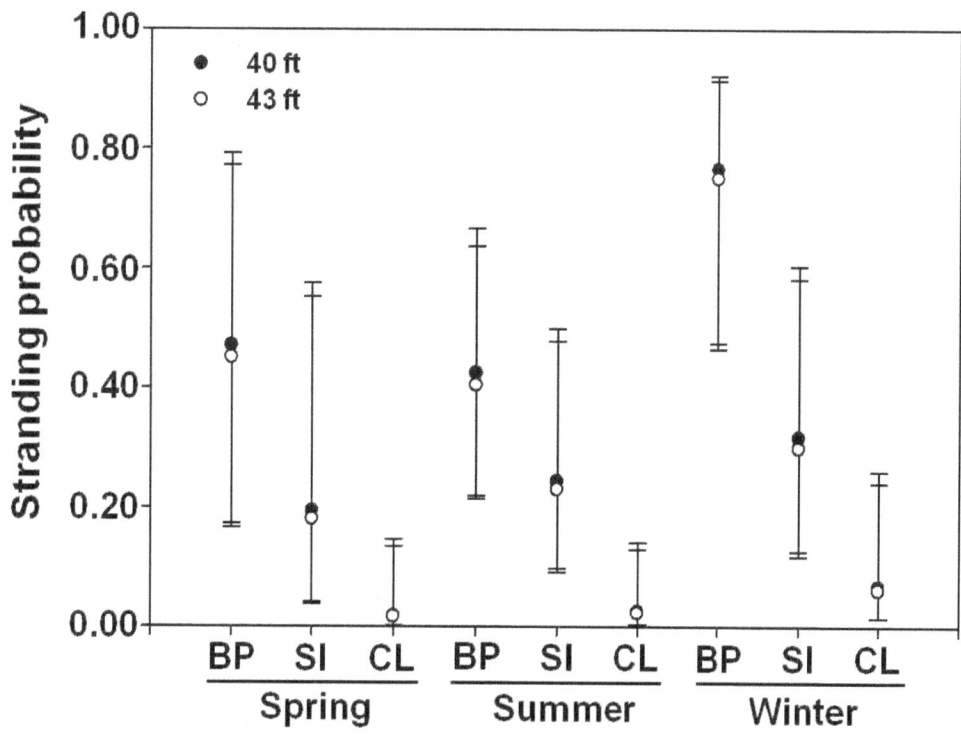

Figure 1. Stranding probability estimates and 95-percent confidence intervals from Scenario 1 in Pearson (2011) using bulk carriers that were traveling downstream. Estimates are provided for Barlow Point (BP), Sauvies Island (SI), and County Line Park (CL) during the spring, summer, and winter.

Section 4.5: Which parameters does the model identify as potentially having the greatest impact (that is, increasing or decreasing) on fish stranding probability?

Based on the information that was presented in Pearson (2011), it was not possible to determine which parameters had the greatest impact on stranding probability. The covariate data were not scaled for direct comparison because some of the values had been squared and/or log-transformed. Pearson's (2011) analyses were not designed to evaluate the data in this manner. His approach generally provided stranding probability estimates under average conditions observed during each season at the three sampling locations. There are statistical techniques that could be used to identify which parameters have the greatest impact on fish stranding probability but that was beyond the scope of the Pearson (2011) modeling objectives as well as our review of the model. Consequently, the importance of model parameters to fish stranding remains a primary source of uncertainty in the LCR and this issue has yet to be directly assessed.

Section 4.6: At what magnitude in value do those parameters begin to impact fish stranding? Do the magnitudes correspond to conditions characteristic of the post-project Lower Columbia River and estuary?

This question is difficult or impossible to answer. Pearson (2011) developed his model using factors that were previously thought to be important in wake stranding of juvenile salmon. The author predicted relatively small declines in stranding probabilities between the pre-construction and post-construction conditions at the sites where data were collected. This finding implied that fish stranding probabilities in the LCR following channel deepening operations might decline very slightly at those sites. We emphasize both the plausibility, but also large uncertainty about these estimates.

Section 4.7: Based on the estimated percentage differences in stranding probabilities for the various navigation scenarios, do the corresponding power analyses (that is, necessary sampling efforts) appear reasonable and appropriate?

Pearson (2011) provided a single example of a power analysis in the section, "Discussion" of his report, and findings for that analysis appeared to be reasonable and appropriate. There were several scenarios, however, for which power analyses were not provided and could not be reviewed. Pearson (2011) evaluated five different ship types, including bulk carriers, car carriers, container ships, tankers, and articulated tugs and barges. As previously discussed, the model forecasted small changes in stranding probabilities between the pre-deepening and post-deepening channels, however, the uncertainty in those forecasts were quite large. Pearson (2011) provided a series of power curves for container ships in figure 3 of his report and discussed that sample sizes of 300 or 400 ship-passage events would be required during the post-deepening surveys to detect the predicted changes in stranding probabilities. The assumptions used to create these power curves were reasonable and appropriate and the analysis seemed to be valid. However, the power analysis appeared to be primarily for discussion purposes only because similar power analyses were not provided for the remaining ship types. It is possible to conduct power analyses to determine the required sampling effort needed for each of the ship types under the various scenarios presented in Pearson (2011), but those analyses were not presented by the author.

Section 5: Alternative Models

Section 5.1: Are there alternative empirical formulations that could be developed to address the overall modeling objectives given the data and information available for developing the Pearson (2011) model?

A Poisson (count) or simulation (stochastic or dynamic) model also could be used to address and quantify fish stranding probabilities in the LCR. Alternative approaches would provide additional information for predicted changes in stranding probabilities. The primary differences between the two models presented by Pearson and others (2006) and Pearson (2011) and a third model, such as a Poisson or stochastic model, is the type of estimates that are generated by each model. Pearson's (2011) logistic (binomial) regression model generated a single stranding probability estimate for each scenario that was examined. Similarly, a Poisson (count) model would generate a single estimate for each scenario, but the estimates would describe numbers of fish stranded, rather than probabilities of stranding. The two models are very much related because the binomial and Poisson distributions also are related. A stochastic (random) simulation model would be similar to Pearson's (2011) model because it would use prior information on fish stranding and environmental changes to estimate potential fish stranding outcomes. A simulation model can provide a time-series of estimates that could incorporate temporal environmental effects, rather than a single point estimate of stranding probabilities. Incorporating stochastic outcomes over a time-series in the model also would provide confidence intervals that are based on a given set of conditions. However, simulation models are complex and best suited for relatively large datasets so additional data collection and modeling efforts would be required.

There are distinct advantages and disadvantages to each modeling approach. The Pearson (2011) and Poisson models are most applicable for the current analyses because of the limited data (see Section 2.1) currently available on wake stranding in the LCR. Pearson's (2011) model provides a clear, concise approach that uses the available data to provide stranding probability estimates that allow the reader to understand how the risk of stranding could change following channel deepening. A Poisson model also would be applicable to the current dataset and would provide estimates of the number of fish stranded under the various scenarios. The advantages of using these models is that additional data collection is not required to provide reasonable estimates, and estimates obtained from each are intuitive. However, the available data were somewhat sparse (see Section 2.1), so estimates from both models would still show large uncertainty.

The simulation model would provide additional insights into the complex interaction among variables related to wake stranding in the LCR, but additional data collection would be required to obtain more reliable model output. The Pearson (2011) and Poisson models were somewhat limited because input data for the covariates generally are average values, which reduces potentially important variability and information. However, input data for covariates in the simulation model include a range of observed values, and the output from this model may provide an additional perspective on wake stranding in the LCR. This capability is the strength of the simulation model, but it is important to understand that the output from the model will be constrained by the dataset. This means that a robust dataset will provide the best output from the simulation model for observing how trends in wake stranding vary throughout time. Additional data collection would be warranted if a simulation modeling effort was desired. For example, multiple years of data collected throughout the entire LCR would provide substantial variability to the dataset, and this information would be most useful for the simulation modeling effort. In recent years, multilevel (mixed effects) models have become increasingly popular as well (Goldstein, 2011) and these models could also be considered if additional data collection efforts are conducted in the future.

Section 5.2: For example, can a simpler empirical model be developed that would meet the overall modeling objectives?

Simpler empirical models could be developed using model selection techniques; however, Pearson's (2011) model was not overly complex and included factors that were previously thought to be important in wake stranding of juvenile salmonids. The Pearson (2011) model provided estimates that compare pre-construction and post-construction channel depths. It is possible to develop simpler empirical models for analysis given the modeling objectives, although it is not clear why this would be desired. For example, we developed a simpler empirical model (Model 1; table 5) by removing the cross-section ratio parameter from the Pearson (2011) model (Model 2; table 5), and model selection found that the simpler model provided better fit to the data (had a lower AIC value). This indicates that cross-section ratio was not important to fish stranding probability. However, using the relatively unimportant factor of cross-section ratio was necessary to the modeling objectives to compare pre- and post-deepening effects on fish stranding. Another approach would be to develop a suite of very simple models that could be used if substantial differences in factors such as ship size and ship speed were expected following channel deepening. For example, if ship speed was expected to increase substantially, then a model could be developed that only included parameters for location (Barlow Point, Sauvie Island, County Line Park), ship speed, and salmon density (Model 4; table 5). Using this model, estimates could be obtained for low speed (pre-construction conditions) and high speed (post-construction conditions) scenarios. This would achieve the goal of using a simpler empirical model (fewer parameters), but our model selection results suggest that a simpler model will not fit the data as well (table 5). The structure of Pearson's (2011) model was appropriate for the given modeling objectives, included information known to be important in wake stranding in the LCR, allowed for comparison between pre- and post-deepening channel depths, and was not overly complex. The use of a simpler empirical model may not account for factors important to wake stranding, thus the use of a simpler model is unlikely to be warranted.

Section 5.3: What would be the corresponding strengths and limitations of such a model in relation to the stated modeling objectives?

The strengths and limitations of the alternative models are discussed in Section 5.2 of this report, so we refer the reader to that section for responses relevant to this question.

Section 5.4: Are there additional data available (for example, data that describe vessel hull streamlining) that might support the derivation of a more complex empirical (or dynamic simulation) model?

Limitations of the existing data are discussed in Section 2.1 of this report, and the simulation model is discussed in Section 5.1 of this report. Additional data needs are thoroughly addressed throughout Section 6 of this report. We refer the reader to these sections for responses relevant to this question.

Section 5.5: Is a dynamic model needed?

The dynamic model, also known as a simulation model, is discussed in Section 5.1 of this report, so we refer the reader to that section for responses relevant to this question.

Section 5.6: Would a dynamic model require more data or different kinds of data?

The data requirements for a dynamic model are discussed in Section 5.1 of this report, so we refer the reader to that section for responses relevant to this question.

Section 6: Additional Studies or Data Needs

Section 6.1: Are there issues concerning fish stranding not addressed by the modeling study?

Pearson's (2011) report provided a useful examination of the potential effects of channel deepening on wake stranding in the LCR given the data available for analysis, but future investigations will be required to address multiple issues regarding this topic. In previous sections, we have thoroughly addressed the Pearson (2011) model and report, including various aspects of the dataset, results, and interpretations. In our view, Pearson's (2011) study was appropriate, and useful for understanding how wake stranding could be affected by channel deepening. However, future studies and data collection efforts will be required to thoroughly understand wake stranding in the LCR. We have identified four areas of study that could substantially improve the future knowledge of wake stranding in the LCR.

These four areas include: (1) spatial examination of wake stranding throughout the entire LCR; (2) additional evaluation of juvenile salmonid behavior and population dynamics; (3) assessing and integrating predicted changes in ship design; (4) assessing and integrating predicted changes in climate on environmental factors known to cause stranding (particularly river flows).

Research on wake stranding in the LCR has primarily focused on locations at Barlow Point, Sauvie Island, and County Line Park, because these locations are known to strand fish and there is a history of data collection at these sites. However, this approach has resulted in a situation where most of the LCR has not been examined or studied. Because of this, there is insufficient data to adequately determine the effects of wake stranding mortality on juvenile salmonid populations in the system. Pearson and others (2008) reported that sites similar to Barlow Point, Sauvie Island, and County Line Park, based on factors such as beach slope and proximity to the shipping channel, comprised only 11 percent of the LCR. This calculation led Pearson (2011) to conclude that "stranding probabilities over much of the LCR would be substantially less than those presented here (p. 22). However, Pearson and Skalski (2007) estimated that 42,605 juvenile salmonids could be killed annually as a result of wake stranding at the three beaches alone. It is important to understand that these estimates and observations are primarily based on data that were collected during the 2004–2005 field studies at Barlow Point, Sauvie Island, and County Line Park. There have been no field studies since that time to quantify stranding at other locations or to validate findings from previous studies. Because previous research has focused on the repeated collection or use of small datasets from discrete locations in the LCR, future evaluations should increase the scope and magnitude of data collection efforts in order to achieve a more complete understanding of wake stranding in the LCR.

The magnitude of wake stranding is intrinsically linked to the number of juvenile salmonids within close proximity to shorelines, so it is imperative to account for behavior patterns and population trends of juvenile salmonids in the LCR when evaluating wake stranding. For example, juvenile salmonids exhibit diel behavioral patterns that may be important determinants of their susceptibility to wake stranding. During 2003, Tiffan and others (2010) used underwater videography to monitor juvenile fall Chinook salmon in the Hanford Reach of the Columbia River, where stranding from dam-related water-level fluctuations commonly was observed. During the daytime, researchers observed that juvenile salmon commonly were found in groups that were actively swimming and located in the upper portion of the water column. However, during nighttime the juvenile salmon became inactive, were less likely to school, and primarily were found in the lower portion of the water column. This led researchers to conclude that nighttime behavior patterns likely increased the susceptibility of these fish to stranding (due to water-level declines) during this period (Tiffan and others, 2010). Wake stranding studies in the LCR seem to indicate that stranding occurred primarily during the daytime in winter and spring, and during the nighttime in summer (Walter Pearson, U.S. Geological Survey, written commun., March 12, 2013). However, because there are still substantial unknowns regarding wake stranding in the LCR, future studies should strive to incorporate diel sampling strategies to further examine this factor.

Trends in population dynamics also should be addressed to better understand juvenile salmonid susceptibility to wake stranding. Pearson's (2011) data showed that subyearling Chinook salmon were the most commonly observed salmonid species at the locations where his studies had occurred. This observation was not surprising. Small juvenile salmonids frequently use nearshore areas because there is adequate feeding opportunity, protection from piscivorous predators, and low water velocities that limit energy expenditure. Once these fish achieve sufficient body size to begin the smolting process, they tend to move farther offshore and migrate downstream quickly. Given these patterns, it would be important to understand future population trends for pre-smolt subyearling Chinook salmon in the LCR. Previous studies support this need. Pearson and others (2008) observed that additional information on fine-scale distribution, abundance, and timing of outmigration of juvenile salmonids in the LCR will be required to optimize predictions from stranding models. This information will be critical for estimating the number of fish that would be susceptible to stranding, the number of fish stranded, and other factors that are important for management decisions.

Research focusing on spatial patterns of wake stranding and behavioral and population trends in the LCR is recommended to better understand the magnitude of wake stranding. In addition, information regarding future predictions for ship design and climate-change impacts on environmental factors also would be useful. Trends in ship development and operation in the LCR are difficult to predict because commerce-related activities are uncertain. However, consultation with shipping experts during future evaluations could be fruitful for developing parameters related to ship-design and ship-speed characteristics. Describing or predicting these trends is beyond the scope of this model review, but would certainly be worthwhile for future data collection and modeling efforts. Finally, contemporary climate science studies have produced a large amount of information regarding predicted alterations to factors such as water temperature, river flow, and water availability in future decades. These data would be very useful in a modeling effort that could illustrate how wake stranding trends might vary in the coming decades if climate change predictions are realized.

Section 6.2: Are there additional scenarios that should be assessed using the model?

As previously discussed, Pearson (2011) provided a worthwhile examination of various scenarios of interest for managers regarding wake-stranding effects following channel deepening. His approach could be easily adapted to address a diverse array of scenarios. However, given the existing data and observations previously discussed in this report, future efforts should focus on collecting additional data rather than continuing to re-analyze the current dataset.

Section 6.3: Based on the review of the current stranding model, its application and results, are there specific recommendations concerning future field studies, or further analysis of fish stranding in relation to channel modification and commercial navigation? If so, what is recommended?

We refer the reader to Section 6.1 of this report for responses relevant to this question.

Section 6.4: Based on the existing studies and results of the modeling efforts to date, how might a follow-on study be designed to address remaining concerns regarding fish stranding?

Ackerman (2002) observed high variation in the number of fish stranded by wakes, and concluded that the discrepancy between his study, Bauersfeld (1977), and Hinton and Emmett (1994) would require a carefully constructed stratified sample design to accurately assess the causes of vessel-wake induced stranding. We concur with Ackerman (2002) and support a study design that uses a stratified random sample of beaches throughout the LCR. The current understanding of wake stranding would be useful for determining which factors should be incorporated into the stratified random design. For example, beach slope and distance to the shipping channel are known to influence wake stranding (Walter Pearson, Peapod Research, written commun., March 12, 2013) so these factors should be a priority for including into the design. Additionally, there is a relatively wide range of channel depths throughout the LCR. Given this observation, beaches could be sampled in association with the range of channel depths that could be used to determine the effect of channel depth on fish stranding at nearby beaches. In this way, existing variation in channel depth and fish stranding may be used to inform how a change in channel depth might alter fish stranding. Although the final factors used for stratifying the beach locations to sample will require some discussion and agreement, we feel much may be learned by applying a stratified sampling design to quantify wake stranding in the LCR. For example, such an approach should provide: (1) a broader survey of the potential for wake stranding of fish throughout the LCR, (2) a better understanding of the variability in stranding estimates, and (3) the relative importance of the various factors involved. The study design also will hold environmental conditions roughly similar across the sampling locations. For example, river flows, water temperatures, juvenile salmon abundance, migration timing, and ship traffic will be similar. In contrast, any or all of these factors may differ greatly in a pre- versus post-construction study design.

Section 6.5: If fish stranding studies were performed in the future, how might the studies be designed to best determine the effects of channel modifications on stranding (for example, pre- and post-dredging)?

We refer the reader to Section 6.4 of this report for responses relevant to this question.

Section 7: Summary

Given the existing data, the Pearson (2011) study provided a comprehensive evaluation of potential pre- and post-construction differences in wake stranding of juvenile salmonids at three sites. However, there exists much uncertainty in: (1) the extent of fish stranding throughout the LCR, (2) the importance of environmental and biological factors to fish stranding, and (3) how future vessel traffic and other factors might interact to influence fish stranding in unanticipated ways. Consequently, even though current information suggests that wake stranding of fish will be reduced by increasing channel depth, there exists much uncertainty and little evidence to support the predicted directional effect on fish stranding. The Pearson (2011) model and report are useful for examining potential changes in stranding probability following channel deepening, but additional research will be required to better understand the magnitude of wake stranding in the LCR. We recommend a stratified random study design that includes locations throughout the LCR and focuses on known physical and biological factors associated with stranding. Additional research also should strive to include predicted changes in ship design, ship traffic, effects of climate change on abiotic and biotic factors, and anticipated trends in juvenile salmonid populations.

Section 8: References Cited

Ackerman, N.K., 2002, Effects of vessel wake stranding of juvenile salmonids in the lower Columbia River, 2002–A pilot study: Report by SP Cramer & Associates, Inc., Sandy, Oregon, for the U.S. Army Corps of Engineers, Portland District, Portland, Oregon.

Bauersfeld, K., 1977, Effects of peaking (stranding) of Columbia River dams on juvenile anadromous fishes below The Dalles Dam, 1974 and 1975: Report by the State of Washington Department of Fisheries, Olympia, Washington, for the U.S. Army Corps of Engineers, Portland District, Portland, Oregon.

Burnham, K.P., and Anderson, D.R., 2002, Model selection and multimodel inference—A practical information-theoretical approach: New York, Springer-Verlag, 488 p.

Emmett, R.L., McCabe, G.T., Jr., and Hinton, S.A., 1993, In-water habitat restoration and juvenile salmonid stranding in the lower Columbia River: Proceedings of the 8th Symposium on Coastal and Ocean Management, New Orleans, Louisiana, July 19-23.

Goldstein, H. 2011, Multilevel Statistical Models: 4th edition, London, England, John Wiley and Sons, Inc.

Hinton, S.A., and Emmett, R.L., 1994, Juvenile salmonid stranding in the lower Columbia River, 1992 and 1993: National Oceanic and Atmospheric Administration, Technical Memorandum NMFS-NWFSC-20, 48 p.

National Marine Fisheries Service, 2002, Endangered Species Act, Section 7 Consultation and Magnuson-Stevens Act Essential Fish Habitat Consultation, Biological Opinion, Columbia River Federal Navigation Channel Improvements Project: Prepared by the National Marine Fisheries Service, Northwest Region, Seattle, Washington for the U.S. Army Corps of Engineers, Portland District, Portland, Oregon.

Pearson, W.H., 2011, Assessment of potential stranding of juvenile salmon by ship wakes along the Lower Columbia River under scenarios of ship traffic and channel depth: Report prepared for the Portland District U.S. Army Corps of Engineers, Portland, Oregon.

Pearson, W.H., and Skalski, J.R., 2011, Factors affecting stranding of juvenile salmonids by wakes from ship passage in the Lower Columbia River: River Research and Applications, v. 27, p. 926–936.

Pearson, W.H., Fleece, W.C., Gabel, K., Jenniges, S., and Skalski, J.R., 2008, Spatial analysis of beach susceptibility for stranding of juvenile salmonids by ship wakes. Final report prepared for the Port of Vancouver, Vancouver, Washington by ENTRIX, Inc., Olympia, Washington, Project No. 4154501.

Pearson, W.H., and Skalski, J.R., 2007, Assessing the loss of juvenile salmon to stranding by ship wakes at three sites along the Lower Columbia River: Report prepared for Entrix, Inc., Olympia, Washington.

Pearson, W.H., Skalski, J.R., Sobocinski, K.L., Miller, M.C., Johnson, G.E., Williams, G.D., Southard, J. A., and Buchanan, R.A., 2006, A study of stranding of juvenile salmon by ship wakes along the lower Columbia River using a before-and-after design—Before-phase results: Report by the Pacific Northwest National Laboratory for the U.S. Army Corps of Engineers, Portland District, Portland, Oregon.

Quinn, G.P., and Keough, M.J., 2002, Multiple and complex regression, in Quinn, G., and Keough, M., eds., Experimental design and data analysis for biologists: New York, Cambridge University Press, p. 111--154.

Tiffan, K.F., Kock, T.J., and Skalicky, J.J., 2010, Diel behavior of rearing fall Chinook salmon: Northwestern Naturalist, v. 91, p. 342–345.

U.S. Army Corps of Engineers, 2003, Columbia River Channel Improvement Project—Final Supplemental Integrated Feasibility Report and Environmental Impact Statement: U.S. Army Corps of Engineers, Portland District, Portland, Oregon, 1998 p.

www.ingramcontent.com/pod-product-compliance
Lightning Source LLC
Chambersburg PA
CBHW080359290526
45791CB00009BA/2935